A Place Called Merkle

Charles Rygg

Illustrated by: Joshua Allen

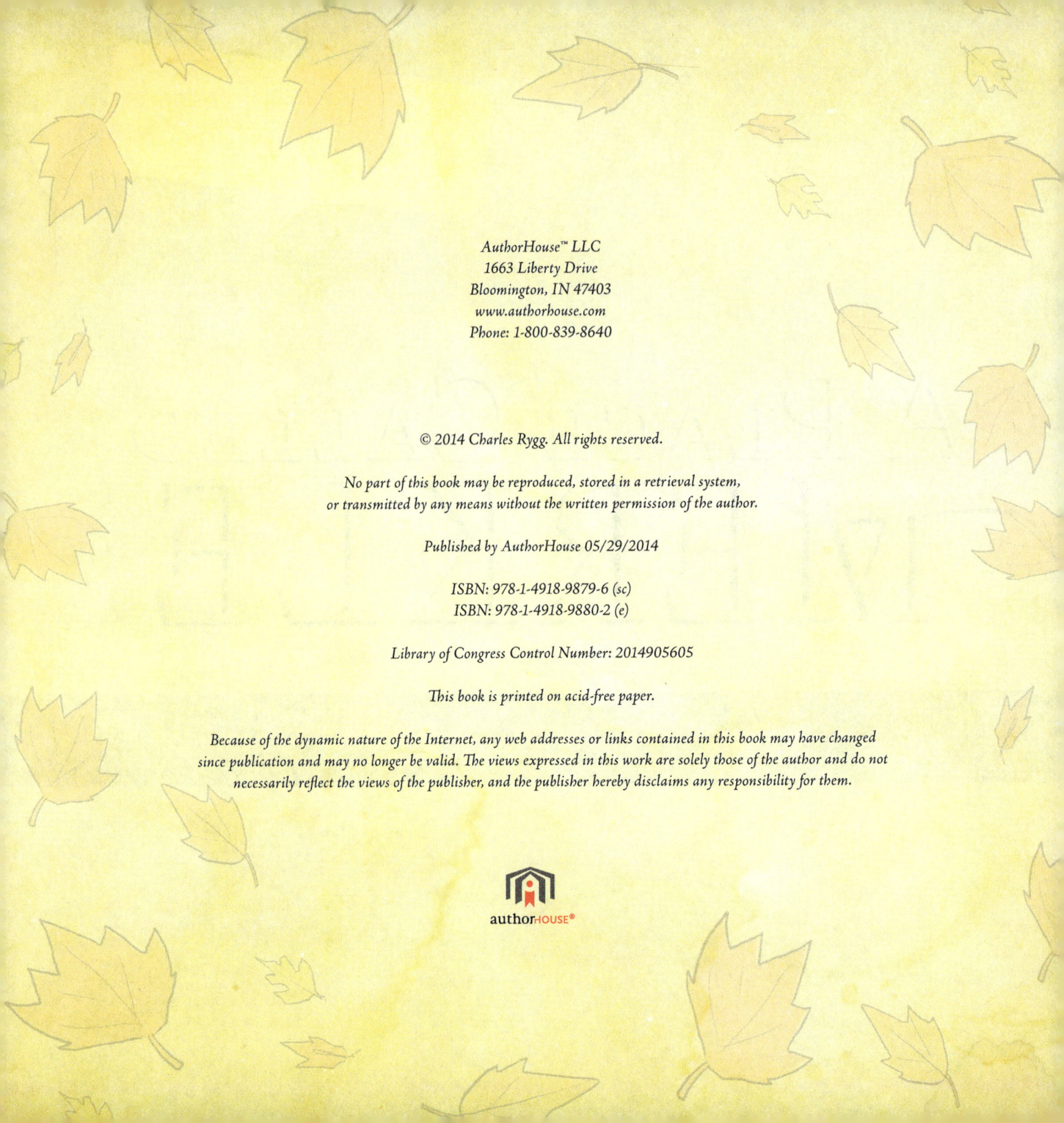

AuthorHouse™ LLC
1663 Liberty Drive
Bloomington, IN 47403
www.authorhouse.com
Phone: 1-800-839-8640

© 2014 Charles Rygg. All rights reserved.

No part of this book may be reproduced, stored in a retrieval system,
or transmitted by any means without the written permission of the author.

Published by AuthorHouse 05/29/2014

ISBN: 978-1-4918-9879-6 (sc)
ISBN: 978-1-4918-9880-2 (e)

Library of Congress Control Number: 2014905605

This book is printed on acid-free paper.

Because of the dynamic nature of the Internet, any web addresses or links contained in this book may have changed since publication and may no longer be valid. The views expressed in this work are solely those of the author and do not necessarily reflect the views of the publisher, and the publisher hereby disclaims any responsibility for them.

A Place Called Merkle

Brrrum, brrrum, brrrum, CRASH! A young deer ran from his hiding place.

"Oh, my gosh! What are they doing?" Button shrieked as he watched a bulldozer pushing over trees. "Why would someone want to do that?" The bulldozer crept closer and closer pushing down trees. "Where am I supposed to live now?"

Turtle replied, "it's moving time again. I've moved three times. Oh' it took me a whole month to move last time," he said as he slowly crept through the bushes.

"I don't want to move," says Button with that saddened look in his big, brown fawn eyes. Button was so frightened, he was shaking all over and his little white tail was flicking up and down.

"In a few days, there won't be anything left," said Turtle. "We have to move, Button."

As the little deer left his home, not knowing where to go, he paused for one last look. "This is the only place I know."

Just then a chipmunk ran up. "You know where you're going?"

No said Button, "and I'm afraid." "Do you want to come with me?" the chipmunk asked because he felt afraid and alone too. "I've heard of a beautiful place that boarders on the Patuxent River, called Merkle. Word has it that all animals are welcome there. And you won't have to move anymore!"

"I guess so," said the trembling little deer.

"What's your name?" asked the chipmunk.

"My name is Button," said the deer.

The chipmunk ran up Button's leg and jumped on his head. "Button! Ha, yes I see," the chipmunk exclaimed as he saw the beginning of the deer's antlers growing.

"Well, I'm Joey," said the chipmunk, "and I'm glad to meet you, Button." And the two new friends started off for the land called Merkle, Button trotting along with Joey riding on his shoulder.

Along the way they came across a cornfield. There was scarcely any corn left, just one patch to be picked, a few ears on odd stalks, and some kernels on the ground remaining from the picker.

"I'm hungry," said Joey.

"All right," said Button. "I could use something to eat too"

"Did you hear that?" said Joey

Nearby a squirrel wrestled with an ear of corn. Snap . . . as the corn came loose from the stalk. Thud, as the squirrel hit the ground with his new prize. The squirrel started digging into the corn. "Man, this stuff is good! Better than the crop they used to grow here."

"Hey!" said the squirrel. "Who are you?"

I'm Button," said the deer, "and up here is joey," he said, motioning to the chipmunk on his shoulder.

"So . . . ANOTHER deer trying to steal my corn! Well, it's not going to happen!"

"No, I wasn't said Button. Button was a little offended that the squirrel thought he wanted to steal his food. But Joey went on to explain. "We're just passing through," said Joey, "on our way to Merkle!" "What's your name," said Button

"I'm Sammy, Sammy squirrel. Where are you going?" asked Sammy

"Someone is tearing our house down, so we're moving to Merkle."

"Aaaah, refugees, huh? Well, nobody's tearing down my house, and if they try, I'll bite 'em on the leg, then I'll give 'em one of THESE," and he swung wildly with his fists, but then turned and ran into a solid chunk of wood with a sign hanging off it. The sign said "sold"

Sammy scared himself so badly that he ran up on Button's back, shaking his tail wildly in a panic motion, alongside of Joey.

"Would you get that tail away from me?" said joey, as he pushed the bushy tail away.

"What is THAT," Sammy cried.

"I don't know," said Button.

"I've seen one before," said Joey. "There was one just like that at our house right before they tore it down."

The three friends all realized at once what that sign meant. The animals could live there no more.

"Oh, my! They're going to tear down MY house TOO! Screamed Sammy, as he fell off Button's shoulder and landed on the ground crying. Sammy didn't want to lose his home any more than Button or Joey wanted to lose theirs.

"Where am I going to live? How will I eat?" asked Sammy.

Button replied, "Why don't you come with us? That's what Merkle is all about."

"Can i? Can I really? Oh thanks a lot guy's!" Then joey and Sammy climbed up on Button's head. Sammy grabbed Button's little button antlers. "Is this how you steer?" he asked. "Go right!" as he yanked on Button's little antler's.

Sammy was so relieved to find not just one, but two new friends, and they all needed to find a place to live.

As the autumn leaves fell, blanketing the woods in a beautiful red, orange and yellow carpet, the three new friends heard a loud rumble. It was a combine that started driving around the field harvesting what was left of the corn in the field.

"We had better stick to the woods and stay out of that thing's way," Sammy quickly found out that Joey was the leader.

"Which way are we going, Joey?" asked Button.

"East!" said Joey.

"How long will it take to get there?" asked Sammy.

Joey replied, "a couple of days, so we had better get going!"

And so now the three new friends walked through the woods together on their way to Merkle. It wasn't long, though, when they heard a distress cry. A mouse ran by, yelling "PHERO! PHERO!" and ran for cover in a dead stump of a tree. Squirrels in their trees started yelling at the intruder, "DANGER! DANGER!"

Who is Phero?" pleaded Button.

A nearby squirrel screamed "CAAAT! You had better RUN!"

Phero, a very large black and grey striped wild cat, was known for patrolling the woods in search of food and often preyed upon squirrels, chipmunks, and other small animals he could catch.

Joey pleaded with Button, "can we PLEASE go? I'm scared of cats!" as the black and brown hair stood up on his back.

"I'm not," said Sammy. The three of us together can take care of him." Sammy hopped up on a stump, "we're making a stand! I can't take this anymore. This ends right here!"

Phero jumped out from the bushes and started running right towards Sammy. Button yelled, "Sammy, get out of the way!" and started moving toward the cat.

Sammy turned and saw Phero running towards him. "AAHH! He's going to eat me! Sammy and joey scampered up a tree. But Button stopped the cat in it's tracks as he made a grunting noise, reared up, and kicked Phero with his front hooves.

"You're not going to eat anybody around here. Now BEAT IT!"

Phero replied, "you can't hide behind that deer all the time . . . and I'll be watching."

Sammy and Joey both yelled from the tree, "yeah, beat it, scram, get lost!"

"C'mon," Button said as Phero crept off into the bushes. Sammy and joey crawled down and both hopped onto button's back. "Let's go get some dinner."

As they began walking through the woods again, they came upon some freshly fallen acorns and started filling their bellies with them. Sammy found a nice, big acorn, and started digging a hole. Button asked, "what are you doing?"

"I'm burring this acorn."

"Why?" asked Button.

"safekeeping for the winter,"

Then Joey asked, "do you ever find them again"

"Well . . . no," said Sammy, but my brain keeps telling me to bury the acorn."

"Well that doesn't make much sense, Sammy, especially since you're not coming back here," said Button

"Would you guys lay off" Sammy whined.

"Hey look. There's some thicket over there. Let's go bed down for the night," Button said. And everybody, exhausted from the threat of Phero, and with a belly full of acorns, thought that was just fine. And as the air started getting chilly, they laid down and snuggled together to keep warm.

Early the next morning, as the sun came through the trees, the guy's set out, stopping briefly to eat acorns, when they came upon a paved road. They stepped out onto it in total amazement.

"Listen to the sound it makes under my hooves," as Button danced around.

Sammy ran out and just starred at the street.

Joey ran across the street and said, "Didn't your mom tell you not to play in the street?"

"But this is so fun," replied Button.

And then, VROOM! "Get out of the way!" Ordered Joey.

"Yikes," yelled Sammy as they ran out of the road. And VRRROOOM, a car went racing by.

"We're never going to get to Merkle if we keep playing around like this," said Joey. And they all agreed they had better get back to business and started back through the woods.

They were making good progress toward their new home and all of a sudden, BOOM, BOOM, BOOM! The sound hurt their ears, and the bushes started shaking in front of them. Sammy and Joey ran up onto Button's back.

"What is that?" cried Joey. But before anyone could even try to answer, all of a sudden, SLAM! A young doe ran right into Button, knocking both Sammy and Joey off his back.

The doe yelled, "RUN!" and all four of them ran through the woods, with Sammy screaming, "I'm too young to die!"

They ran and ran, and when they finally stopped, Button asked, "What was that?"

"Hu..Hu..Hunter," replied the young doe, out of breath from the dash across the forest.

"What's your name," asked Button.

"Noalani," the pretty doe answered. "What's yours?"

"I'm Button and this is Sammy and Joey.

"It's not safe here," said Noalani. "We had better go."

Would you like to go with us?" asked Button.

"Where are you going?" asked Noalani.

"We are going to Merkle," said Sammy.

"Yeah," said Joey, "it's a place so beautiful, where all animals can be free."

"Are there hunters there?" asked Noalani.

"No," said Button. Merkle is a special place for animals, and no hunters are allowed to go there."

That sounded just great to Noalani, and she was happy to have someone to show her the way to a safe place. So the four of them set off together and continued their journey to the land called Merkle.

The sun began to set and the foursome decided to keep moving through the night.

"It looks like it might storm," said Sammy, "we had better move along. We should try to get across the creek before the storm."

It wasn't long before rain started to fall and streaks of lighting lit up the sky. The rain just didn't want to stop. It came down harder and harder, and the creek started to overflow the banks.

The yellow glow of cat's eyes pierced from the bushes as Phero waited for the right opportunity to strike.

"We'll have to cross at that beaver dam over there," said Button. Follow me, single-file. Button led the pack, with Joey and Sammy in the middle and Noalani at the rear, making sure everyone was accounted for.

About half way across Phero leapt from the bushes and ran towards Noalani to try to get to Joe, but Joey jumped onto Noalani's leg just in time, as Phero skidded by. Failing to catch Joey, Phero tried to grab at Sammy but Noalani gave Phero a push knocking him into the flooded water and washed him away.

They carefully finished crossing the rest of the dam. "We better find some cover," said Joey.

"I can't take all this excitement," said Sammy, "my fur is going to fall out," as he plucked some hair from his head. "Let's find a pine thicket to bed down for the night."

The four set out early the next morning, singing a song to pass the time, when Noaloni stopped and said, "have you guy's noticed that we're the only ones making noise? Something must be wrong."

"Do you smell that?" said Button, "Let's try to keep our heads down.

BOOM, BOOM!! Bullets started whizzing by. "RUN!" Sammy and joey jumped onto Button's and Noaloni's backs, and they sprinted through the bushes. "I think we're safe now," panted Button, all out of breath

The four calmed down and trotted along, when they came upon another paved road and started walking down it."Fenno road. Are you sure this is the right way?" asked Sammy.

"I think so replied Joey

Then they came upon a sign with a picture of geese on it. "What does it say? Asked Sammy.

Merkle Wildlife Sanctuary!" said Noalani.

You mean, we're here?" asked Joey.

"Yes said Button. And they all started running down the road towards the sanctuary. Just then a car came by as they were running through a cornfield. The car slowed down near them, and they all stopped in their tracks. A passenger raised up his camera to take a picture, Sammy squealed, "Oh my! What are they doing? DUCK, DUCK! It's another hunter! He's going to shoot!" Sammy began running around in circles hopping on Button's and Noaloni's heads screaming . . ."GET DOWN, GET DOWN!"

Joey leaped at Sammy and wrapped his little chipmunk body around Sammy's neck. "Settle down, Sammy. It's ok. They're not hunters," said Joey.

"You mean they're not trying to hurt us?" whimpered Sammy.

"No. That boy is just taking our picture," said Joey

"Gee, Dad. There sure are some nutty animals around here," said the boy in the car.

"There sure are, son replied the father, and the car drove off.

Then the four followed a long white fence down the road and it opened up into a large field. They gazed out at the beautiful fields of winter wheat and herds of deer grazing. Hundreds of geese filling the fields and ponds full of all sorts of ducks.

"Oh, it's going to take a long time to meet everybody," said Sammy.

There was also a building, and thru the glass Sammy could see people staring out of the windows, but he was no longer afraid because he realized they weren't hunter's either. They just wanted to watch the animals.

"Isn't it beautiful?" cried Noaloni, with a tear in her eye.

"I just can't believe it!" said Button, looking around with wonder.

We're finally home," said Joey

CPSIA information can be obtained at www.ICGtesting.com
Printed in the USA
BVOW10s2307270814

364486BV00007B/198/P